At Home with Science

Bump! Thump!

How do we jump?

Written by Janice Lobb

Illustrated by Peter Utton and Ann Savage

KING*f*ISHER

KINGFISHER
Kingfisher Publications Plc
New Penderel House
283-288 High Holborn
London WC1V 7HZ
www.kingfisherpub.com

First published by Kingfisher Publications Plc 2000
First published in paperback 2002
10 9 8 7 6 5 4 3 2 1 (HB)
1TR/0400/FR/128JWAD
10 9 8 7 6 5 4 3 2 1 (PB)
1TR/0201/SCPC/FR/128MA

Created and designed by Snapdragon Publishing Ltd
Copyright © Snapdragon Publishing Ltd 2000

A CIP catalogue record for this book is available
from the British Library.

ISBN 0 7534 0429 X (HB)
ISBN 0 7534 0498 2 (PB)

Printed in Hong Kong

Author Janice Lobb
Illustrators Peter Utton and Ann Savage

For Snapdragon
Editorial Director Jackie Fortey
Art Director Chris Legee
Designers Chris Legee and Rob Green

For Kingfisher
Series Editor Emma Wild
Series Art Editor Mike Buckley
DTP Co-ordinator Nicky Studdart
Production Caroline Jackson

Contents

About this book

Did you know that science is happening when you're running around outside, playing ball or riding your bike? This book is all about the exciting things going on inside you when you take exercise. When you look at your body in action, you'll be amazed to discover how it works.

How?

What if?

Why?

Which?

Where?

Hall of Fame

Archie and his friends are here to help you. They are each named after a famous scientist – apart from Bob the duck, who is a young scientist just like you!

Archie
ARCHIMEDES (287–212BC)
The Greek scientist Archimedes worked out why things float and sink while in the bath. According to the story, he was so pleased that he leapt out, shouting 'Eureka!', which means 'I've got it!'.

Frank
BENJAMIN FRANKLIN (1706–1790)
This American statesman carried out a famous (but dangerous) experiment in 1752. By flying a kite in a storm he showed that a flash of lightning was actually electricity. This helped people to protect buildings during storms.

Marie
MARIE CURIE (1867–1934)
Girls did not go to university in Poland, where Marie Curie grew up, so she went to study in Paris, France. She worked on radioactivity and received two Nobel prizes for her discoveries, in 1903 and 1911.

Dot
DOROTHY HODGKIN (1910–1994)
Dorothy Hodgkin was a British scientist who made many important discoveries about molecules and atoms, the tiny particles that make up everything around us. She was given the Nobel prize for Chemistry in 1964.

See for yourself!

1 Read about the science of your body when you're running around outdoors, then try the 'See for yourself!' experiments to discover how it works. In science, experiments try to find or show the answers.

2 Carefully read the instructions for each experiment, making sure you follow the numbered steps in the correct order.

3 Here are some of the things you will need. Have everything ready before you start each experiment.

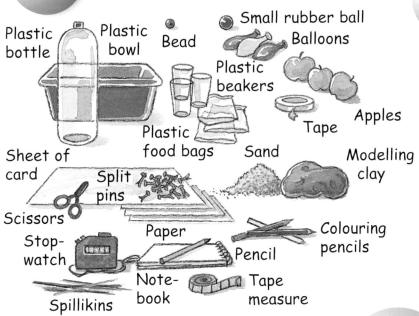

Plastic bottle
Plastic bowl
Bead
Small rubber ball
Balloons
Plastic beakers
Plastic food bags
Tape
Apples
Sheet of card
Split pins
Sand
Modelling clay
Scissors
Paper
Colouring pencils
Stop-watch
Pencil
Note-book
Tape measure
Spillikins

4 Safety first!

Some scientists took risks to make their discoveries, but our experiments are safe. Just make sure that you tell an adult what you are doing, and get their help when you see the red warning button.

Amazing facts **WOW!**

You'll notice that some words are written in *italics*. You can learn more about them from the glossary at the back of the book. And if you want to find out some amazing facts, look out for the 'Wow!' panels.

Look out for useful tips!

Have fun!

What are bones for?

Our bodies contain over 200 different bones of various sizes. Together, they form a framework called the *skeleton*, which props us up from the inside and gives us our shape. Without bones, we would look soft and shapeless, like slugs or jellyfish. Bones are made of a tough living material, and protect the soft parts of our bodies from being damaged or squashed. They also provide an anchor for our *muscles*, which are joined on to them and move them about.

> What do you call a skeleton that won't get up?

> Lazy-bones!

Body guards

Feel your head. Your skull is like a helmet which covers and protects your brain.

Muscles in your face open and close your jaw bone.

Skull

Jaw

Your ribs form a cage which protects your heart and lungs.

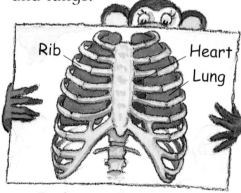

Rib

Heart

Lung

Feel your ribs move as you breathe in and out.

Instead of bone, some parts of your body, such as your ears, are supported by *cartilage* which is softer and more flexible.

Ear

6

See for yourself!

1 Try to count the bones in your fingers. Each thumb has two bones and each finger has three, which makes a total of fourteen finger bones on each hand.

2 Now see if you can count the same number of bones in your toes. Which toe has only two bones, like your thumb?

3 Use a tape measure to find out which bone in your arm or leg is the longest. In your leg, it is usually the thigh bone, or femur, which stretches from your hip to your knee.

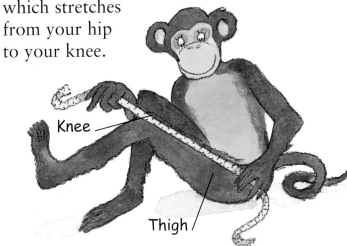

Knee

Thigh

No bones about it!

Not all animals have skeletons made of bones. Mammals have them, as do fish, amphibians, reptiles and birds. Other animals have a different kind of skeleton to support and protect them. A crab or a lobster has its hard parts on the outside - it has an *exoskeleton*.

For strong bones, eat foods with plenty of calcium and protein.

7

How do I move about?

Every movement that your body makes uses skeletal muscles. There are over 600 in your body. Without them, you couldn't run, walk, eat, smile or speak. As your muscles change length, they pull on your bones and make your body move. Each muscle is fixed to two or more bones by strong strings called tendons. To tell the muscles what to do, your brain sends messages along your *nerves*. When babies are first born, they find it difficult to control their muscles. We all learn to do this as we grow older.

Which parts of the body come from the sea?

Mussels!

Working in pairs

At the top of your arm is your biceps muscle. One end is fixed to a bone in your shoulder, and the other end is joined to a bone just below your elbow.

As your biceps contracts, or gets shorter, it pulls your arm up and your elbow flexes, or bends. The biceps cannot stretch on its own.

As the triceps muscle at the back of your arm contracts, it pulls the arm down and your elbow straightens.

BENDING YOUR ARM

Biceps muscle contracts

Bone

Elbow flexes

Triceps stretches

Biceps stretches (relaxes)

Triceps contracts

See for yourself!

1 See what some of your muscles can do. Hold your arm out straight. Flex your biceps to bend your elbow. Then use your triceps to straighten it again.

2 Bend your hand up and back. Feel which muscles are contracting and relaxing. They are smaller than your upper arm muscles.

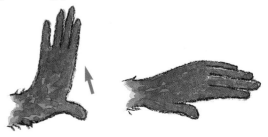

3 Now bend and straighten a finger. The muscles you use to do that are even smaller than your hand muscles.

4 Make your eyes look up and down. There are little muscles behind the eyeball. They have good control, so that we can watch things.

Muscles in your face change your expression by making your skin move.

Look up, smile!

Look down, frown!

WOW! Pumping iron!

The more you use your muscles, the stronger and bigger they grow. You also need to have good protein and vitamins in the food you eat. Some kinds of exercise, like weight-lifting, give people very strong muscles.

Regular exercise keeps you fit!

Can my bones bend?

Have you noticed that when you move your leg, it is the knee in the middle that lets it bend. Hard bones above and below stop the leg from bending anywhere else. The place where the knee bones meet is called a *joint*. There are many other joints in the body, which allows the skeleton to change position. Most of them allow bones to move freely, some give a little movement, and a few do not move at all. Joints can be large or tiny. The smallest joints of all are inside your ear.

Where do you find your hippies?

At the top of your leggies!

Moving parts

Knees and elbows are hinge joints. They open and close like a door in one direction only.

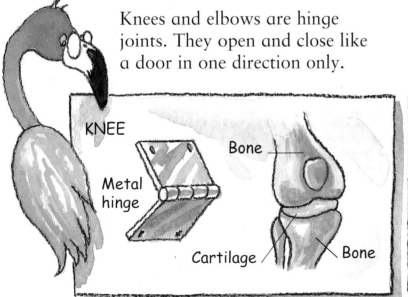

KNEE

Metal hinge

Bone

Cartilage

Bone

Shoulders and hips are *ball and socket* joints. They allow arms and legs to swivel in several directions.

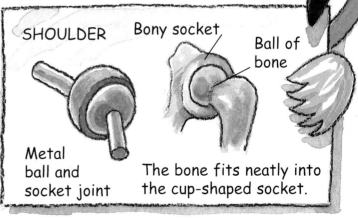

SHOULDER

Bony socket

Ball of bone

Metal ball and socket joint

The bone fits neatly into the cup-shaped socket.

See for yourself! ✋

1 To make a model of an animal, draw some shapes on to card for the head, upper and lower body, hands and feet, upper and lower arms and legs.

2 Cut out the shapes and join them together with split pins, which allow the parts to move about.

3 Put your model in different positions, and see if you can copy them yourself. If you fix a piece of string to the top of its head, you can make it into a dancing puppet.

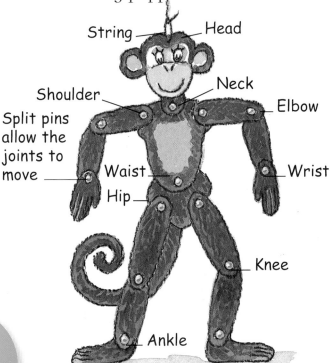

String — Head

Shoulder — Neck

Elbow

Split pins allow the joints to move

Waist — Wrist

Hip

Knee

Ankle

Oiling the joints!

WOW!

Like a piece of machinery, a joint needs to be kept lubricated to work properly. Inside the joint, there is a slippery liquid which helps the bones slide freely over each other. The surfaces of the bones are smooth and shiny, so that they do not catch on each other. Joints become stiff and sore if they dry out or the bones get rough.

Hinge joints help to bend your fingers too.

How do I pick things up?

What part of the body do you use when you pick up a ball? A dog would use its mouth, a bird might use a foot, but a monkey, ape or human can use one hand on its own. Many animals have *limbs* which are used to do things, but humans are able to do much more than any other animal by using their hands. To grip things with one hand, we have an opposable thumb. This means that the fingers and thumb can bend towards each other and meet on either side of an object.

What did the head say to the hands?

You're all fingers and thumbs!

A good grip

Using a finger and thumb, you can pick up and hold a ball or a tiny seed.

Small muscles in your hand move your finger and thumb.

Rodents, like this squirrel, don't have thumbs. They have to use two paws.

A parrot's back toe goes in the opposite direction to the other toes, so it can use it like a thumb.

12

See for yourself!

1 See how you would manage without any hands like a fish. Try playing the party game called 'bobbing for apples'. How hard is it to pick things up using only your mouth?

2 How would you manage as a hamster? Tuck your thumb into your hand, and try picking things up without using it. You can't do this with one hand only.

A hamster has no thumb.

3 Using your thumb and forefinger, you can pick things up quite delicately. Try the game of 'spillikins' to see how good you are.

4 Monkeys and apes can use their feet as extra hands. Can you do that too?

A monkey can use its big toe to grip a branch.

WOW!

Brain power

Animals which use their hands and feet to move things about generally have bigger brains than other animals. They are more intelligent. Humans, monkeys and apes are the most intelligent mammals, and parrots are the most intelligent birds.

Could you use chopsticks without using your thumb?

How high can I jump?

When you jump in the air, you always come back down again. This is because a *force* called *gravity* pulls your body towards the ground. Gravity is also the force that gives us our weight. Although your body weighs you down, your muscles are able to push you upwards. To do this, they have to provide a force which is stronger than gravity's pull. How high you can jump depends on how strong your muscles are for your size.

Yes! Houses can't jump!

Can you jump higher than a house?

Using energy

To jump, you need *energy*. Your muscles use *stored energy*, which comes from the food you eat.

When you are jumping, the energy stored in your muscles is turned into moving energy.

Food

Stored energy

Muscles

Moving energy

Stored energy

Moving energy

14

See for yourself!

1 Drop a small rubber ball on to a hard surface from waist height. If it stores energy, it will bounce up again when it lands. How high does it bounce?

2 Now make a ball of modelling clay the same size as the rubber ball. Drop it on to a hard surface and compare each ball's bounce. Does clay store energy like rubber?

3 Make a mini trampoline by fixing a piece of balloon over the end of a strong plastic cup, using a rubber band. Drop a large bead on to it and see how high it bounces.

The trampoline stores energy which makes the bead bounce.

4 Drop the bead from the same distance on to a hard surface. Does it bounce as high as it did from the trampoline?

WOW!

Jumping in space

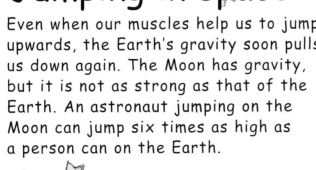

Even when our muscles help us to jump upwards, the Earth's gravity soon pulls us down again. The Moon has gravity, but it is not as strong as that of the Earth. An astronaut jumping on the Moon can jump six times as high as a person can on the Earth.

Be careful where you bounce your ball!

How do I keep my balance?

Why does a flamingo lift only one leg?

If it lifted the other one, it would fall over!

Keeping your balance means not falling down. You need to keep your balance when you are standing or moving about, because at any time the pull of Earth's gravity could make you fall over. For you to stay upright, your weight needs to be supported directly underneath. You use your *senses* to tell you how to do this. Your eyes tell you where you are, and your ears have a very important part to play in keeping you steady.

Getting dizzy

Inside your head, behind the ear that you can see, is your inner ear. Its sensitive hairs can tell if your head turns, nods or is upside down.

As you move, liquid inside the ear moves these hairs and sends messages to the brain.

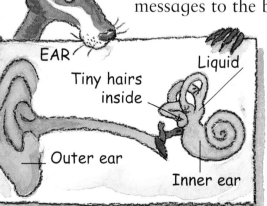

EAR

Tiny hairs inside

Liquid

Outer ear

Inner ear

You get dizzy if you spin around fast, because your inner ear gets confused and cannot tell you where your head is. When you try to move, you will fall over.

16

See for yourself!

1 First test your balance by walking along a straight line. Is it easier if you look at the line, or if you look ahead ?

2 At the end of the line, see how long you can stand on one foot without wobbling. Then try this again with your eyes closed.

3 Now spin around for a few seconds. Try walking and balancing again. Do you think your ears or your eyes are more important for keeping your balance?

Be careful not to spin too quickly.

WOW! Great team work!

Your brain acts as the leader of a team. It takes in information from all your senses, and tells the muscles which ones need to work to support your weight. Their team work gets better with practice.

Stabilisers on a bike help you to balance.

17

Why can't I fly like a bird?

A bird has four limbs. It stands on its back legs, like us, but its front limbs are specially designed, or adapted, for flying. We have arms instead of wings, but even if our arms were changed into wings, we still couldn't fly. Our bodies are not built in the right way. Birds have strong wings with very light bones. They also have feathers to help to lift them off the ground, and a *streamlined* body shape which moves smoothly through the air.

What do you call a person who thinks he can fly?

Plane crazy!

Hollow bones

Birds have very light bones, which contain bags of air. These help them to float in air and on water. Our bones are too heavy and solid for flying or floating, and our breast muscles are not strong enough to lift us into the air.

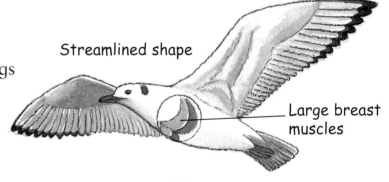

Streamlined shape

Large breast muscles

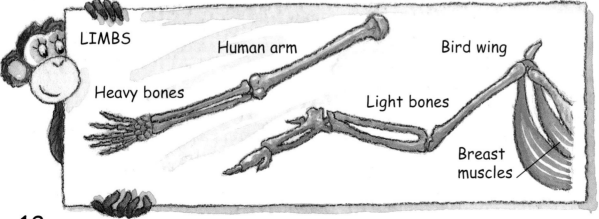

LIMBS

Human arm

Heavy bones

Bird wing

Light bones

Breast muscles

There is very little weight in a bird's wing. Most of it is made from bone, skin and feathers. The large breast muscles which flap the wings are not in the wings at all.

See for yourself!

1 Birds flap their wings to fly. They also glide. Try making paper planes, and see how far you can make them travel.

Centre of paper

Fold top corners in toward centre

Fold corners in toward centre again

Fold in toward centre once again

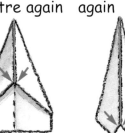

Step 1   Step 2   Step 3   Step 4

2 Does your plane glide better if you feather the edges?

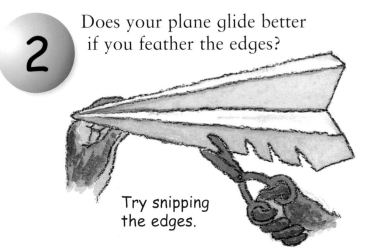

Try snipping the edges.

3 Does a short, wide plane glide better than a long, narrow one? Do tiny planes fly better than big ones?

Decorate your plane with markers or coloured pencils.

 WOW!

Water wings!

Some birds have wings that are too small to allow them to fly. Penguins swim by 'flying' under water. Ostriches use their wings to help steer themselves as they run. Kiwis' wings are so small, they are hidden under their feathers. But the moa, a huge bird which is now extinct, had no wings at all.

Penguins use their wings like flippers.

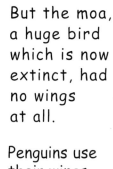

A bird's feathers also help it to keep warm.

How do I breathe?

What did the chest say to the nose?

Let's get some fresh air!

When you breathe in through your nose or mouth, you are taking air into your *lungs*. All the working parts of your body need *oxygen* from the air to help you use the energy in food. The air passes down your *windpipe* in to your lungs, which pick up the oxygen and pass it into the blood. Breathing changes the air in your lungs, so they always have a good supply of oxygen. When you breathe faster and more deeply, you get more oxygen. Holding your breath makes you feel light-headed because you are not getting enough oxygen.

Air balloons

Your lungs are rather like thin balloons of air stuck to the inside of your chest. They are soft and spongy.

Muscles between your ribs and below your lungs are able to make your chest move out. This helps to

suck new air into your lungs. When these muscles squeeze your chest in, the old air is pushed out.

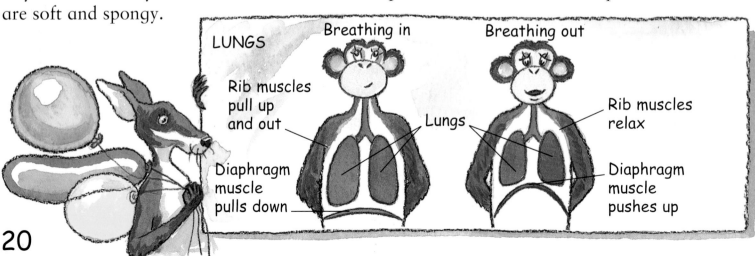

LUNGS

Breathing in

Rib muscles pull up and out

Lungs

Diaphragm muscle pulls down

Breathing out

Rib muscles relax

Diaphragm muscle pushes up

See for yourself! ✋

1 You will need a medium-sized plastic bottle, some tape, a handful of sand or rice, a strong plastic bag and a balloon. Ask an adult to cut the bottom off the bottle.

2 Put the balloon inside the top of the bottle and stretch the neck of the balloon over the bottle's neck. Fix it in place with tape. Fill the plastic bag with sand, and fix it inside the other end of the bottle.

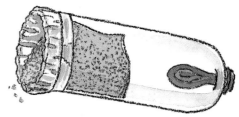

3 Now tip out the sand. The bag should stay inside the bottle. This is like your chest after you have breathed out. Pull the plastic bag out, and the balloon should start to get bigger. This is what happens in your lungs when you breathe in.

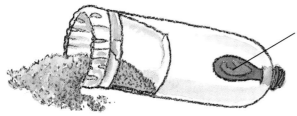

A little air goes into the balloon

4 The more you pull the bag, the more air goes into the balloon. This is like taking a deeper breath, when more air goes into your lungs.

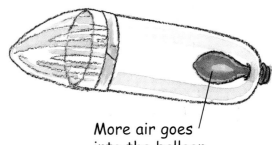

More air goes into the balloon

WOW!

Hiccups!

Just above your tummy, there is the diaphragm muscle. Sometimes, if you eat or drink too quickly, it gives a series of little jumps called hiccups. The diaphragm contracts and air rushes into your lungs, making a clicking noise in your throat.

Coughs and sneezes push air out fast.

Why do I get out of breath?

When you exercise, the hard-working muscles in your body make *carbon dioxide*. Too much of this is bad for you, so your blood takes it to your lungs, and you breathe out to blow it away. You know how fast to breathe because the brain has a kind of smoke detector. This senses how much carbon dioxide is in your blood, and makes you breathe faster when you need to. The faster you get rid of carbon dioxide, the more oxygen you get into your lungs.

What bird is always out of breath?

A puffin!

Using energy

When you are resting, your muscles don't need much oxygen and don't make much carbon dioxide. You can breathe slowly.

Running around uses more energy, so you need a lot of oxygen and make a lot of carbon dioxide. You breathe quickly to change the air in your lungs.

When you can't get enough oxygen, even by *panting*, your muscles may keep going without it. They make *lactic acid* instead of carbon dioxide. This makes you tired and gives you a *stitch* in the side.

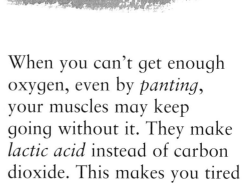

See for yourself!

1 Rest quietly for one minute, and count how many times you breathe in and out. If you are small and fidgety, you will take more breaths than someone bigger and quieter.

2 Hold your breath for a few seconds, then see what happens to the next breath.

Count one, two, three in your head!

3 Run around for a few minutes. Then sit down and count your breaths in one minute again. You will be breathing faster than when you were resting. See how long it takes to get back to 'normal'.

Puffing and panting

WOW!

When a dog pants, it may not be because it has been running around, but because it is too hot. When it pants, water evaporates from its tongue which takes its body *heat* away. Dogs, and many other mammals and birds, pant to cool down instead of *sweating*. When animals pant to keep cool, they do not take deep breaths.

You take in about 0.5 litres of air with each normal breath.

Why do I get hot and sweaty?

What goes in pink and comes out blue?

A swimmer on a cold day!

Have you noticed how hot you can feel after exercise? Your muscles use stored energy from food. When they have finished using the energy, they turn it into heat. In cold weather, this heat helps you to keep warm. If you are running around a lot, your muscles make more than you need, and you feel too hot. When your body wants to lose heat, blood comes closer to the surface of your skin, causing it to go red and produce sweat.

See for yourself!

1 On a cold day, your hands feel cold. See how good your muscles are at making heat. Jump up and down ten times. Are your hands still cold?

Cold hands

2 If they stay cold, repeat the jumps again and again. How many times do you have to jump up and down before you feel warm all over?

Your muscles make extra heat.

Temperature control

Sweat comes through little holes, called pores, in your skin, and makes it wet. The water *evaporates* - it escapes into the air and takes heat with it. This cools your body down.

When you are cold, tiny muscles in your skin contract and pull up the hairs on your skin, trapping air to keep you warm. This gives you goose pimples.

Your muscles are so good at making heat that they can do it when you don't move around. This is what happens when you *shiver* to keep warm.

Sweat | HOT

Pore

Muscle

Sweat gland

COLD | Goose pimple

Skin

Muscle

Blood vessel

Your body tries to keep at an even temperature of 37°C or 98.6°F.

Good grooming!

WOW!

When monkeys and apes sweat, the water evaporates from their skin, leaving flakes of salt behind. This helps to stop germs growing on the skin. You can see the monkeys picking these off when they groom one another. Our sweat is salty too.

Remember to warm up slowly before you exercise.

Why does my heart go thump?

Have you ever felt your heart thumping and wondered what it was doing? It was working hard to keep your blood moving around your body through little tubes called *blood vessels*. Your blood carries food energy and oxygen to your muscles so they can keep going. It also takes away carbon dioxide from your muscles, so that they don't feel tired. The more you run around, the harder your heart beats to pump blood to your muscles.

Can I take your pulse?

Haven't you got one of your own?

Pumping blood

Your heart works like a pump, squeezing the blood inside it out to your muscles and lungs. Between thumps it relaxes to fill up with blood again.

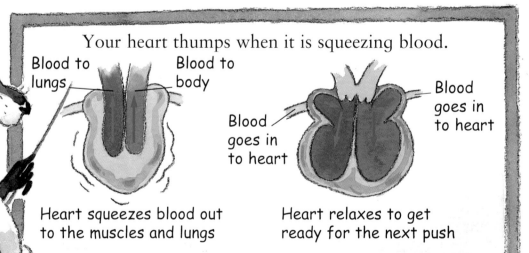

Your heart thumps when it is squeezing blood.

Blood to lungs

Blood to body

Heart squeezes blood out to the muscles and lungs

Blood goes in to heart

Blood goes in to heart

Heart relaxes to get ready for the next push

See for yourself!

1 If you put the fingertips of one hand on your other wrist, just below your thumb, you can feel a little throb in your wrist every time your heart thumps. This is your pulse.

You can feel your heartbeat in your wrist.

2 While you are sitting quietly, try counting the number of throbs you can feel in one minute. If you can't feel your pulse yourself, get a grown-up to count for you.

You can also find your pulse on your neck under the jaw bone.

3 Run around for a while, then test your pulse again. It should feel faster, because your heart is working harder. Try counting your pulse several times, and then compare the results.

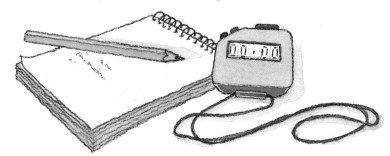

Big hearted

WOW!

You might expect big animals to have fast heartbeats, but it is just the opposite. Big animals have slower heartbeats than smaller ones. Your heart beats faster than that of a grown-up. The heart of a tiny mouse or a canary beats about one thousand times a minute.

Your heart is about the same size as your clenched fist.

Why do I yawn?

When you are tired, bored, or are ready to go to sleep, you yawn. Your muscles need oxygen and lots of a sugar called *glucose* to work well, but if they have been working very hard, they can run short. Your muscles slow down and feel weak, because they don't have enough energy left. When they try to work without enough oxygen, they make a waste substance known as lactic acid. This makes your muscles ache, and when it collects in your blood, it gives you a stitch. When you are tired you need to rest.

Why does a bicycle fall over?

Because it's two-tyred!

Open wide

Sometimes, when you are resting, your blood does not move along fast enough. A big yawn gives it an extra push along back to your heart, so that it can be pumped out again.

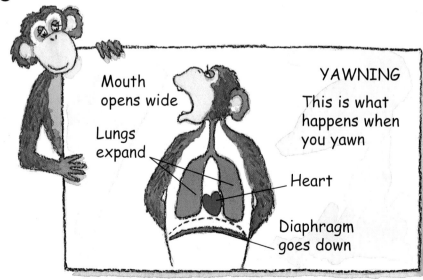

Mouth opens wide

Lungs expand

YAWNING

This is what happens when you yawn

Heart

Diaphragm goes down

You also yawn when you are bored, or you have not been breathing deeply enough.

See for yourself!

1 See if your yawn is catching. Choose a moment when you are sitting down with your friends and family. Don't tell them you are about to do an experiment!

People and animals may yawn when they are ready to go to sleep.

2 Try yawning when someone is looking at you. If nothing happens, wait a little while, then yawn again. Sometimes you can get everyone in the room yawning with you.

Yawning may also suggest 'Why don't you go to sleep too?'

WOW!

Beating forever

You may get tired, but your heart is made of a special type of muscle which never gets tired. It starts contracting before you are born and keeps going until you die. If you live to the ripe old age of 80, your heart could beat over three thousand million times.

YOURS FOREVER

We're tired now! Goodbye!

29

Body quiz

1 Which bones protect your heart and lungs?

 a) The spine
 b) The skull
 c) The ribs

2 Which muscle bends your arm?

 a) The triceps
 b) The forceps
 c) The biceps

3 What type of joint is your shoulder?

 a) A hinge
 b) A ball and socket
 c) A nut and bolt

4 What pushes you up when you jump?

 a) Your muscles
 b) Your nerves
 c) Your bones

5 What do penguins use their wings for?

 a) Swimming
 b) Flying
 c) Catching fish

6 What does yawning do to the blood?

 a) It makes it move more quickly
 b) It makes it move more slowly
 c) It makes it stop moving

7 What is carbon dioxide?

 a) A gas
 b) A joint
 c) A muscle

8 What does your body need from air?

 a) Carbon dioxide
 b) Oxygen
 c) Enzymes

9 When does your heart thump?

 a) When you are hungry
 b) When it fills up with blood
 c) When it squeezes blood

10 Where does sweat comes from?

 a) Spores
 b) Pores
 c) Tear ducts

Answers on page 32

Glossary

Ball and socket
A joint where the round end of one bone turns around freely inside the cup-shaped end of another one.

Blood vessels
A network of tubes carrying blood from the heart, around the body and back to the heart.

Carbon dioxide
A waste gas made by muscles and other cells after they have used up all the energy in glucose.

Cartilage
A substance which gives support to parts of the body. Cartilage is not as hard and stiff as bone.

Energy
The ability to do work. Energy can be changed from one kind to another.

Evaporate
To turn surface liquid to vapour without boiling.

Exoskeleton
A hard shell, often jointed, on the outside of an animal. It protects the animal, and is where its muscles are attached.

Force
A push or pull which changes something's movement or shape.

Glucose
A type of sugar which most cells use for energy.

Gravity
The pull from the Earth which makes things fall downwards.

Heat
A type of energy which can warm things up, and make them melt, evaporate or boil.

Joint
The place where two (or more) bones come together. It may allow the bones to move or it may be fixed.

Lactic acid
A waste substance made when there is not enough oxygen to use all the energy in glucose.

Limbs
The jointed parts of an animal's body which are used for movement.

Lungs
A pair of spongy bags with thin walls, inside the chest, where oxygen is taken into the blood and carbon dioxide is given out.

Muscles
Parts of the body which can change length. There are different types of muscle in the heart, alimentary canal, and attached to bones.

Nerves
Fibres which carry information from the senses to the brain, or orders from the brain to the muscles.

Oxygen
A gas in the air. People, animals and plants need oxygen to live.

Panting
Breathing quickly, either to get more air, or to lose heat.

Senses
Special structures, linked by nerves to the brain, which allow the brain to keep a check on what is going on outside and inside the body.

Shiver
When muscles produce extra heat by making lots of quick little movements.

Skeleton
A hard structure inside an animal's body which supports and protects it.

Stitch
A sharp pain in the side, caused when the body runs short of oxygen and builds up too much lactic acid.

Stored energy
Energy that is contained in things (eg. a stretched or squashed piece of rubber). Stored energy can be converted into other forms of energy.

Streamlined
Shaped so that air or water flows smoothly over the surface. Usually narrow at both ends and more rounded in the middle.

Sweating
Producing sweat, a watery, salty liquid, which comes from pores in the skin's surface. As sweat evaporates, it cools the skin.

Windpipe
A tube which takes air from the throat to the lungs.

Index

Answers to the Body quiz on page 30
1 The ribs. 2 The biceps. 3 A ball and socket.
4 Your muscles. 5 Swimming. 6 It makes it move more quickly. 7 A gas. 8 Oxygen. 9 When it squeezes blood. 10 Pores.